SC[illegible] GARDENING

A collection of articles
on Spiritualist thought and life

Richard Burridge

Published in 2023 by FeedARead Publishing

British Library C.I.P.

A CIP catalogue record for this title is available from the British Library.

Cover illustration: *A Nosegay of Roses, Marigolds, Larkspur and a Bumblebee.* Oil on canvas. Rachel Ruysch. 1695. Private collection. The image is in the public domain.

Cover design by Kevin Taggerty

Foreword

Richard Burridge was taken to Kingston Spiritualist Church and introduced to Spiritualism by his father-in-law in the 1950s, but it was 30 years later that he seriously investigated it for himself, joined a development circle and eventually became a healer. His love of philosophy grew, he read widely and also developed the skill of inspired writing, communicated by the spirit world.

In the 1990s he joined the committee of Ealing Spiritualist Church, where he had trained as a healer and from 1997 started writing thoughtful articles as a frontispiece to the regular church events list. The articles contained in this book were written and first published between 1997-2012. Richard was Church President from 2003-2012 and often made entertaining and thoughtful philosophical addresses from the platform.

His writing reflects his very personal and sometimes quirky take on current events, the meaning of life, and Spiritualist thought. He also observed nature and loved gardening. He was a man who tried, above all, to live his philosophy. Richard was often heard to say that he "wasn't ready to leave the planet yet", but sadly had to leave us for the higher life in January 2020.

This small collection is part of his legacy and is dedicated to his memory. The footnotes are an editorial addition to explain references, mainly to contemporary events.

Lynn Burridge

February 2023

Contents

Foreword 3

Articles

Appendix

Don’t worry what’s ahead.
It’s only the future.

I write this on a day when our hopes that the weather was returning to a semblance of summer have been jolted by yet another thundery cloudburst, and I read that the strawberry and cereal harvests will no longer be as good as we once hoped.

Our ancient ancestors would have responded “the gods are angry”, and we now and with less certainty ask “is the planet trying to tell us something?” Well, maybe it is, but our technology and manufacturing abilities have complicated our lives to the point where there are no longer clear coherent answers to our self-doubting questions.

We all have more of the “things” of life, even those at the lowest level of our social order, but as politicians found to their cost, we remained dissatisfied and unable to feel good. When we have cushions for our chairs and food for our tables such dissatisfactions are rooted in our hearts and are not really assuaged by material offerings.

For many, the emotional perceptions have become blurred, and they can no longer differentiate between happiness and pleasure, and a sharpened acquisitiveness allows some to feel only envy. Any sense of feeling happiness at another’s pleasure, or even pleasure at another’s happiness has become an alien impulse.

There can be grounds for supposing that life teaches us that which we most need to learn, and that our circumstances are guiding us towards better understandings. Let us, then, see our problems as our learning programmes and our situations as spiritual gardens which we can tend and in which we can make beautiful things grow. Let us also recognise that others are tending their criticism, which not only deters, but also reveals our own limitations and prejudices more fully than we might realise.

So, if there is a message from Mother Earth it may only be that we have to keep on changing. Many of the good old ways, which were pretty grim and repressive for most of us, have been abandoned and the new-found freedoms have gone to many heads. Well, so maybe we haven't got it right first time (not that this was the first time anyway) but we can change it again if it still isn't good for us, until the day when we can feel unconditional joy in our heart at the happiness and pleasures of others.

July 1997

Looking both ways

At the beginning of another year, we tend to emulate the old Roman god of the winter solstice or new year and look both backwards and forwards. He, Janus, had the advantage of having a second face at the back of his head; but we have to make do with a mixture of memory and anticipation.

The public events of last year[1] - I mention only the change of government and the death of a loved royal figure - caught almost all of us in the great waves of emotional outpouring that swept us along at the time.

By now, most of us will accept that we over-reacted, that our lives were not changed to the extent that we thought, and see that we surrendered our individuality to the pressures of the mass emotionalism. Being Spiritualists, we are more than averagely sensitive to waves of public emotion even if we deny being psychic, and our response indicates that we have started to make progress but that there is still more work to be done.

I would think that when we have made those advances, we will begin to seek a more detached attitude that will allow us to consider constructively "how does this really affect my (spiritual) life?", and to reflect on the universal laws that might have applied to the event.

And what of the new year? I guess that most of us will only change a little. External events will continue to catch us by surprise, until we have developed the ability to evaluate,

---

[1] A general election in May 1997 resulted in a landslide victory for the Labour Party under Tony Blair, and in August 1997 Diana, Princess of Wales, died in a car accident in Paris.

without wishing for the happy ending that our prejudices so often demand.

January 1998

That which is nearest

The old injunction that we should turn our hands to "that which is nearest" of the many tasks and opportunities that surround us, gives us a guidance for more than our duties to the world.

"That which is nearest" is also good advice regarding our spiritual lives and the attention we should pay to what is probably a near constant stream of educating experience devised for our progress. We tend to apply ourselves, with laudable diligence, to meditation, mediumship, healing, prayer or some other chosen activity; and seldom think that Life itself is leading us forward into greater understanding.

It is my suspicion - I will leave it to you to find your own stronger conviction - that we pay insufficient attention to our every-day experiences in our relationships with family and friends, and that it is through these that we learn the joys and pains of life.

It does seem that the lessons of life that we need to learn are drawn to our attention by the experience of pain, the pain that also helps to indelibly impress them on our memories.

You may quite fairly ask "is pain necessary for our progress?" and I can only answer that it seems so at the present level of achievement. Perhaps a time will come when it will be sufficient for us to have the hazards of life explained to us, but we are not as yet pre-disposed to accept advice, because the ego part of our mind assures us that we can stand life on its head.

Unless we pay attention to the pain that we cause others, they are unlikely to minimise the pain that they cause us. We are all here to learn, and the pain of learning may be one thing, but needless and thoughtless repetitive pain that only dulls the senses is entirely another. Let us remember that we are here to help each other, particularly those who are nearest.

April 1998

A hell of a responsibility

At a recent Sunday service the speaker observed that our Fifth Principle[2] was "a hell of a responsibility", if we would pardon her expression, and I agreed with her. Further thought only confirms my agreement.

Whichever way I throw the thought it lands on its feet with cat-like agility and reveals yet another aspect of its significance.

Obviously, the Principle is telling us that we cannot lead irresponsible, feckless, selfish lives and expect a generous and cheerful forgiveness from life when the scores are added up – sometime, somewhere, the mess that you made will have to be cleared up; presumably by you.

There is also the consideration that wilful departures from our intended paths of experience and learning invoke the negative effects of the Natural Laws, and thus provide the painful and miserable experiences that should bring us back to our senses and lessons – we have responsibility for our hells, for we have made them.

Furthermore, even if we have avoided "those things which we ought not to have done", we can still make a hell in our minds: a hell of either endless anxiety or imagined guilt. To be eternally fretting that every aspect of our lives will meet with the approval of our neighbours, and even our friends, will leave us in a hell of indecision as we try to guess what their verdict will be. We can make a duty of every act and then nothing is done for joy or for self-expression.

---

[2] The Fifth Principle of Spiritualism is "Personal responsibility". See page 84

I have, myself, too often nursed the guilt of off-hand thoughtless remarks, only to find that when I finally summoned up the courage to offer something of an apology, my erstwhile victim had already forgiven me and knew of my regret. In some instances, they had entirely forgotten the incident, and I made a further fool of myself by reminding them of it.

The thread through all these thoughts is that *we* do the making: we make our own hells more often than they are made for us. Which does not mean that we should stop living and sit glumly in a corner, but rather that we should think a bit more about the possible disadvantages that could be attached to our current dream or ambition. The old maxim advises "never pray for something unless you really want it, because you might actually be given it".

God, Spirit, or Providence, whichever name you care to use, provides for our needs, but we actually want more than just our needs – some cake with it would be nice! When help comes in unexpected ways we often refer to such gifts as god-sends. But have no doubt that God, or Providence decides what would suit his purpose for us, and that they really signal God's-ends.

July 1998

Perfect is as perfect does

Perfection is not a spiritual terminus at which progress and striving stop. Any concept of having arrived implies that stagnation will set in, and I for one cannot accept that the highest planes of existence are a sticky foetid swamp. Sorry, but anyone who hopes that they will be able to rest and loll around for ever is in for a disappointment. I'm sure that the very first stifled sigh or yawn will attract the quiet murmur: "There's a little job that we think you could do for us".

Perfection is all right as far as it goes, but I'm sure that it's better to look upon it as a Clapham Junction where you have the possibility of starting on any one of a number of new journeys. After all, even a perfected human being may not be Creation's answer to everything. And anyway, you will not be the very last one to achieve perfection (or I hope not) so there will be others to coach, and it won't end there either.

Communications from the spirit world never talk of perfection; all they ever say is that they are a little ahead of us on the path of life and give no hint of any concept of completion. The path seems infinite, and if this is too awesome to contemplate at our present level of development, then perhaps it is not only less daunting but wise to look where our feet are treading, rather than stumble as we gaze into a veiled distance.

The path is all we really have apart from the burdens of materialism, prejudice and sentimentality. Let's remember to enjoy the scenery even when the going is rough. Let's be grateful for companionship, for hands that steady us when we are stumbling, and for the moments of realisation when we can put down a burden and leave it behind us for ever.

Our beliefs are not constructed to offer a swansdown comfort for the languid. Christopher Robin can see nanny's dressing gown on the door but yank the door open and you might just catch the Infinite listening at the keyhole.

October 1998

The Living Truth

The human race has a complex and confused relationship with the truth. One would think the truth to be a fact or principle that we should acknowledge and respect, but all too often we give it a little twist or bias to help it justify our purposes, and truths that we find unacceptable we largely ignore. Even the eternal truths that are proclaimed from the ancient religions, even if originally unsullied, have become distorted in translation or interpretation and no longer provide a sure foundation for a reasoning mind. If one is going to have faith in more life-affirming concepts than death and taxes, it should be a faith in what one knows to be true.

The form of the knowing has to be that inner heart understanding that is beyond external confirmation or negation. I grant that one has to be ruthlessly honest with oneself to separate heart knowledge from wish fulfilment and prejudice, but such honesty is the only way towards living the truth. The living truth is what you find within yourself, and not what has lain gathering dust on someone else's shelf. After all, if it's been gathering dust, he can't have used it much. It is only a living truth if you're living it, and it's only truth at all if founded in your own experience or that of those dear to you.

Modern life has fragmented into many differing strands, any insistence on conformity now only begs the question "with what?" and the unravelled answer will usually be "with my prejudices". We've had enough of conformity, self-expression is now the thing, and we'll probably go too far overboard for it, but responsible self-expression is a large part of what we are here to learn.

The challenge then, that we all face in life, is to express the living truths that we find within ourselves; and we should do this to remind others that they too know such things, and that

KINGSTON NATIONA

Villiers Road, Kingst

Affiliated to the Spiritualist National Union (SNU)
Reg. Charity No. 1160074
PRESIDENT: Mrs Bernadete May
SECRETARY: Mrs Ann Morrice
TREASURER: Mrs Catherine Rumsey
CHURCH MOBILE: 07503 405007
BOOKING LINE: 07780 474440
Email: kingston.spiritualist@yahoo.com
Website: www.kingstonsc.net facebook

PROGRAMM

Listed Event

Sat	1	**Open Platform** *OPEN TO A*
Sun	2	**Sunday Divine Service**
Mon	3	**Monday Evening of Mediums** followed by Spiritual Healing
Wed	5	**Spiritual Healing**
Fri	7	**Open Spiritual Awareness Cir**
Sun	9	**Sunday Divine Service**

SPIRITUALIST CHURCH

n upon Thames, Surrey, KT1 3AR

HEALING bv donation
Mon.: 8.45-9.15pm & Wed.: 2-4pm (side door) (pets allowed)
MONDAY EVENING OF MEDIUMSHIP £4 (£3.50 mem)
SPIRITUAL AWARENESS 1st & 3rd Fri £6 (£5 mem) aged 18+
GUIDED MEDITATION 3rd Wed £6 (£5 mem)
OPEN PLATFORM (trainee mediumship) 1st Saturday aged 18+
Working Mediums £6 (£5 mem) Congregation £3
EXPLORING Holistic Healing £7 (£6 mem)
Events open to all. Please enquire about CLOSED CIRCLES

E for JUNE 2024

Are Open To All

LL	2-4pm	Lesley Hamilton
	11am	Karen Pyle
hip	7.30pm	Riki Davies
	2 - 4pm	
:le	7.30pm	Lynn Rose
	11am	TBA

living them not only draws subtle benefits into life, but also rewards with a sense of fulfilment and purpose. Remember though, that teaching by example must be no more than that: the other person remains free to accept or reject the lesson. After all, are they ready to learn it? Perhaps, even more to the point, are we ready to wait while they learn it in their own way and time?

January 1999

Teaching the kids to have respect

It's common enough these days to see a carpet of broken glass around a bus shelter or phone box, and I think we all initially react by thinking "if I caught them doing it, I'd really make sure they never did it again". Well, I have to say that we would all too certainly fail in our intention: in fact, we would be doing almost exactly the wrong thing, because it might be said that we were committing another violence.

The impulse to damage or break things is born of an inner anger and not from an over-exuberant sense of fun. The act of destroying something gives an outlet, albeit only temporary, for deep-seated anger at some earlier injustice. The punishment that we would have dealt out would only add to that sense of injustice. Maybe they wouldn't do that again, but they might well do something worse instead. What has through most of history been called respect has, in fact, been no less than a fear. Respect for parents has too often been only a fear of the punishments that they might inflict. Real respect is born of an appreciation of qualities that one admires, cherishes, and hopes to express in one's own life.

How then might we teach our children to live with real respect as an integral keynote of their lives? Remember that we cannot induce it by fear of pain; remember too, that it must be a part of their very nature, instilled in them from babyhood, because to start later is already too late.

It would seem to me that as we can only teach by example, we must change ourselves before we can hope to change the next and future generations. If so, then we must literally show our children respect, a greater respect than many currently enjoy, for they themselves are not treated with a proper respect; so they have no appreciation of the mutual benefits that would accrue to all. All very difficult in a world where parents spend long hours at work and fathers may only be seen at weekends. Difficult too, in a society where too many children are conceived thoughtlessly and without the intention of creating a stable loving relationship in which a child would feel cherished and secure.

Even in this country it is scarcely more than a hundred years since small children were treated as cheap expendable labour, without any thought for their health or welfare, and such things still occur in parts of this world. A lot of progress has been made in the century now ending, and social conditions have improved perhaps even beyond the hopes of the early reformers; but the further changes now needed are more personal, for we now have to change hearts as well as minds.

We have to become able to express love less conditionally. We have to learn to love life more fully, and to love ourselves less critically, for only then will we be able to express a proper love for our children, a love that will show that we cherish and respect them and find joy in their lives. Then they will learn to have greater respect for us, for bus shelters, and most importantly of all, for themselves.

April 1999

Not for the faint-hearted!

Spiritualism can sometimes seem to be an "all things to all people" religion, but those who are seeking a sure and definite end to their tribulations will be disappointed at our concept of eternal progress and the learning and potential pain that that implies.

The concept of "Rest in Peace" may imply no more pain, but also suggests no more of a lot else besides. Pain is not an absolute requirement of progress, but while we take too little interest in our own spiritual advancement, the learning has to be thrust upon us. Book-learned knowledge is no real substitute for experience, for it is only lodged in our earthly brains and not in our hearts. It does seem that only what we have felt in our hearts is indelibly recorded, and that our brains can forget seemingly more than they ever knew.

Eternal rest can mean an end to eternal progress and the choice is living or mouldering. Once we have reached the stage of appreciating that positive living can minimise the pains of experience, we can accept eternal life as a joyful adventure. I grant that the early stages of progress can be extremely grotty, but we are at that time not only learning but also unlearning the false concepts that either we dreamt up ourselves, or were led to believe.

What we are inching towards is an acceptance of reality and of life as we experience it. What we have to learn is that it is not we who make life happen: after all, it was already fully functioning before we were born and will continue after we've left the planet again, for it is life that makes us happen. Because some activities and experiences are possible for us, we tend to believe that by choosing those paths we have made them happen. It is rather like thinking that we actually made an apple, when in fact we only picked it off a tree.

Eating fruit is fine and you're meant to enjoy it, but we also have to eat our spiritual vegetables, and like the children we still are, we "don't like greens". An unbalanced diet of life also leaves us with deficiencies – deficiencies that will have to be corrected before we can continue the spiritual progress that is truly our birthright. So try to enjoy life, the experiences are actually good for you!

August 1999

No hype, just the reality

The razzmatazz of the celebrations[3] has died away and we are now facing what was lauded as being an exciting new era that would bring radical improvements to our lives. But my own appreciation is that the material aspects of our lives are becoming less secure, with greater affluence for some and greater uncertainty for the many.

We are, in effect, generally being required to assume greater responsibility for our health, our finances and quality of life. However, I do not detect a similar call from the orthodox religions that we should take individual responsibility for our spiritual wellbeing. The requirement is still that we should conform, though there is some softening of attitudes as the great and good find themselves impaled on their own points of principle. The politicians want us to grow up and priests want us to stay dependent (on them), and the resulting overall message is confusing.

In fact, the prime requirement is that we grow spiritually: not just because it will prepare us for our future life in the spirit world, but because it will greatly affect our lives here and now on the physical plane. Every spiritual truth that we discover changes our attitudes to other people, our expectations from life, and the way that we conduct ourselves. We can in that way, and possibly only in that way, really take responsibility for our own lives in a way that lifts and improves the lot of all mankind.

Material aims may well bring pleasure, but pleasure is a transient thing that will soon need repetition and the repetition

---

[3] 31 December 1999 marked the start of worldwide celebrations to welcome the new Millennium – the year 2000

causes it to cloy. Fulfilment comes from being happy in whatever you are doing, however ordinary or mundane. Happiness itself often seems a will-o'-the-wisp, but that is because so few of us have managed to differentiate happiness from pleasure. Real happiness is that state of mind that enables us to accept the vicissitudes of life calmly and to know that we as individuals are more lasting and more important than our material possessions.

January 2000

The times are a'changing

We are Spiritualists because we already believe in, or are seeking, a caring and beneficent force within Creation. We hold ourselves to be such a part of Creation that our spiritual progress is a part of the universal progress and believe that nurturing that progress is our true purpose and responsibility.

We must therefore seek to play our part in the ordering of the changes that are taking place in the social structures of our civilisation. Not for us the disdaining of merely material changes as being beneath our interest, for we have to remember that we are "in the world" to experience it, even if we do not accept that we are only "of the world". We must endeavour to ensure that Caesar renders unto us the things that are ours.

As befits a time of transition into a new astrological age[4], we are quite inundated by all the changes taking place. The speed is such that we may suspect that we are in the presence of a juggler, but we are assured that all is for the better, or at least materially so. Spiritually it is still every man for himself, but that was always so because no one becomes spiritually better except by his (or her) own thoughts and efforts.

The Aquarian age has been heralded as an era of greater spirituality, but current signs are that we are not necessarily moving into a period of increased leisure and welfare. Spiritual progress has only normally come as a result of a certain level of tribulation, and we may yet be given opportunities to make significant progress.

---

[4] We are said to be moving from the astrological age of Pisces into the age of Aquarius. Astrologers do not, however, agree on when the Aquarian age will start, or even if it has already started.

Spiritualism has never been a nannying belief offering a diet of warm milk, biscuits and a pretence that it never really happened. It requires us to gain understanding and discernment through our experiences so that we can say “I did make that mistake once, but I learned not to make it a second time”.

Life requires us to have a little courage, but we only need sufficient to take the very next step of our life’s journey.

September 2000

As a matter of fact

The world exists, or it is at best our experience that it exists, and it is experience that determines our concept of life and being. The common trap, and we all tend to be caught by it, is to make our experience defining: "I have seen it, I can tell you all about it and please don't tell me that it could be otherwise!"

Experience and perception are not the precise and scientific tools we take them to be, and we are endlessly selecting from the information that our senses provide. So do not forget that when defining something we are defining with the limitation that matters will be no more than we have said. None of which deters the experts from offering categorical opinions on the afterlife, psychic phenomena or spirit communication, even though the concepts are limited by our presently inhabiting physical animal bodies.

We should be always pressing to see beyond the limitations that we have ourselves imposed. Does the concept appeal to our sense of justice? Does the answer allow progress to a greater understanding? Does the reason admit the existence of unconditional love? Without these criteria and others that you can fashion for yourself, you are allowed to express dissatisfaction. Any pretence that you would not understand a proper answer allows you the challenge: "Well, teach me until I can."

Despite the limitations, there are general experiences that we believe to be universally true. We recognise that there is a beneficent force extending to all forms of life, which guides, nurtures and, where necessary, heals. We find that it is possible to order one's life into a harmony with that force. We receive communications from those who have already passed beyond this life, communications that assure us that life is longer and has a greater purpose than material values can measure. The communicators also tell us that we can best co-operate with the beneficent force by guiding, nurturing and healing in our turn; and that we should seek to avoid hurting or hindering.

Life's challenges frequently do not allow that we can resolve a situation without some hurt or obstruction, for our lives now have a complexity that seldom allows simple and ideal solutions. The chosen solution will all too clearly demonstrate our consideration for the other person or creature. Is there anyone who wishes that they were treated with less consideration? Hard to imagine, really. We all long for some appreciation, care and understanding.

If, as individuals, we wish to feel the earthly expression of the beneficent life force, then we have to play our part in bringing it about. We then become bound together by that interplay, and become a part of each other and, literally, human kind.

January 2001

Reflections on 9/11

The events in New York and Washington[5] have challenged all of us with "what if me, what if my family, what if a friend?" questions, and our responses can tell much about ourselves. Are we able to face even the first question, that of such a thing coming within our experience, or is it too awful to think about?

Paradoxically, to ask "how can God allow such things to happen?" only tells about our limited personal concept of God; but to ask "how can people commit such acts?" may tell us more about the realities of God's creation, for such people are a part of the totality of life. What we have to recognise in such acts is that the human potential to behave more destructively than the animals is the price for being able to rise above the animal level of life into an awareness of moral issues and values.

Animals, too, are capable of expressing love and compassion just as we do, so if we are to be their exemplars and inspiration, a function that Spirit insists is our role in creation, then we will have to do better than they. Not easy, you might well say, and I could only reply that if it were easy it would have little spiritual value.

Modern life is a maze of responsibilities, prior agreements and perceived moral standards, all obscured by our prejudices and self-interests, but we are seldom deterred from demanding both justice and the right to determine what would constitute justice. Modern justice may take proof and retribution seriously, but often seems less ardent when resolving the reasons that prompted the act. We are all better at criticising

---

[5] This refers to the four suicide terrorist attacks that took place on the World Trade Centre in New York and three other sites in the USA on 11 September 2001, commonly called simply "9/11"

others than we are at improving ourselves (no change there, then); but it is only in changing ourselves that there is any hope of improving the world.

The maze is of our own making, and we can only begin to negotiate it when we have a higher viewpoint. Until then, and perhaps not even then, there are no simple absolute solutions, and we can only express our highest level of understanding. I'm sure that Shakespeare's "To thine own self be true" demands that we ever seek the highest and best in ourselves, for only then can we be true to others.

The pundits may have said that the world has changed following the events in America. Our answer has to be: "That was not the final change. We're working to make the next change positive and for the highest good."

September 2001

Subjective – Objective?

The ways our minds work and the ways we think often seem to leave us torn between our feelings (subjective) and our observations of the external world (objective), and we are left having to choose between the two views.

I believe this quandary is implicit in being a human being and that we should accept and even use the challenge to enlarge and enlighten our lives. As Spiritualists, we have agreed that progress is open to everyone though there is far less agreement about what constitutes progress, which may be what happens to us while we are busy trying to make our lives happier (and yes, I know that I'm paraphrasing John Lennon). The external objective world shapes our lives more frequently and more profoundly than our subjective feelings are ready to acknowledge, and the uncompromising "You have the illusion of free will" from Colin Fry's Magnus[6] gains a deeper significance.

The old injunction to "be in the world, but not of the world" applies to our considerations when we can accept that worldly matters are often only learning programmes intended for our progress; and that once the progress has been achieved, probably without our conscious awareness, we have little more need than the comfort of familiarity for the material trappings.

The next question is short and easy to ask: "So, who is arranging all this external objective world for us?" The answer will be longer, and harder to accept. In two simple words – we do: obviously almost a *reductio ad absurdum*, but it is the grain

---

[6] The medium Colin Fry had recently carried out a demonstration of trance mediumship at Ealing Spiritualist Church, during which his spirit guide, Magnus, made the remark on free will, quoted here.

of gritty truth that brings a pearl into existence. We are prompted by our spirit guides, our spirit and earthly friends and by our own souls to seek encounters in our external objective worlds that will (or should) bring us to greater understanding and wisdom.

Why? – and the answer predates advertising by several million years – because you're worth it. Your individual progress requires a major investment to make it happen. It needs the love of all those around you, both those with and those without physical bodies. Very often it needs so much love that those around you have to hurt themselves and appear as enemies just so that you can learn a truth. Can you be grateful for their sacrifice? Or will you just go on hating them?

Forgiveness will come more easily if you have learned the lesson that they materialised for you, and don't doubt that there was a reciprocal lesson for them. Forgiveness without the lesson may be noble, but will only beg the further question: "Do we have to go through it all over again?" The answer has to be "Yes" – but I'm sure you knew that anyway.

May 2002

Once more, with feeling

The five physical senses that give us our awareness of the material world are extremely useful tools to have in what we call the "real world", but they are only really suited for practical tasks like placing nails and using hammers to drive them into a piece of wood. However, once we get to the more subtle tasks involving feeling and emotions and keeping a relationship on a positive plane, more subtle senses are needed. Most of us are on less firm ground in these situations and a few more senses than the basic five would come in very handy.

If we are to develop these newer senses then we have to enter another plane of life where the central organ seems to be the heart, not the brain. Caring and loving come from the heart, which doesn't make the brain redundant. Hearts are often too extravagant and living in idealist worlds, so the brains have to provide the stability that avoids the otherwise ensuing chaos. Traditionally the Divine Spark within us is thought to have its home in the heart, but that does not mean that spirit promptings and initiatives are extravagant and idealized, merely that they are so strong that we can over-respond to them.

To grow into wisdom, we have to learn to be wise masters of ourselves. In learning to love and take a caring interest we will learn to seek what is best for that person and what will most help them overcome the difficulties and lessons that confront them. In that way we'll be helping them to become wise in turn, wiser than if we first endeavour to satisfy their whims and fancies.

Each generation has to learn that balance between heart and brain, letting neither one act at inappropriate moments, and there may even be moments when the only wise course of action is to do nothing but wait until your friend or partner has faced up to the challenge facing them. Little presents will only distract them, and you may well have to say “I desperately care about your problem but only you can make yourself happy again.”

Spiritualists may initially be amazed at the reality of spirit communication, but once they have accepted that it is natural and normal to their lives, their interests turn back to this world, and they wonder how they might better play their part in the universal progress. Much as we like helping other people (at least somebody says thank you), we should not neglect our own progress: learning to listen to our own intuitions, hearts and brains with skill and trust will aid us through both our lessons and those of people near and dear to us.

Although we are often told how wonderful the next life is, we never seem in any hurry to get to it. My first father-in-law (a Spiritualist healer) during his final earthly days said to me: “I thought I had so much more to do.” I guess most of us will echo that.

May 2003

Happiness is…

Making sense of one's life seems ever more difficult in the modern world as there are additional distractions that still appeal despite our awareness of their transient nature and their ultimate failure to provide any lasting sense of satisfaction. This sense of ultimate disappointment comes because we have mistaken pleasure for happiness. One can be happy with things as they are; but pleasure requires an effort either by oneself or others, and as the pleasure fades, we need a repetition of the effort.

Usually, we are trying to substitute a pleasure for lack of real happiness, most often caused by the lack of any sense of purpose or fulfillment in our lives. Happiness is, of course (far more) a state of mind thing rather than a state of circumstances, and some sense of having made a choice seems implied. What we chose was not to be happy or unhappy, for surely no-one actually chooses to be unhappy, but we have chosen to be selfish rather than unselfish, or at least to be overly selfish. We can have clear ideas of what the world owes us, but little notion of what we might owe the world.

In exploring our individuality and personal uniqueness and in the competitive world of work we can lose sight of our fellowship with those around us and even the fragmentation of family groups by the need for modern work and housing requirements may have added to this. Continuous employment seemed to provide a pseudo-family of fellow workers, but even that is vanishing with endless reorganizations and "temping".

It seems to me that what we lack nowadays is a sense that we are doing something, or even anything, for someone who will appreciate our efforts with an expression of gratitude or some return of goodwill or effort. When last in the supermarket did you say "hello" and smile at the check-out person? Such simple small gestures will bring a response from them and an unspoken acknowledgment that you share the problems of struggling with the difficulties of earth plane life. Alternatively, you could have just complained about the length of the queue and left them feeling even more fed up with their rather boring job.

We have to regain our sense of fellowship; after all, it's a small planet as planets go, and we could even learn to enjoy many more aspects of our lives. Any task performed with the sense of having done it for someone and of having done it with care will give greater satisfaction.

We receive from life to the extent that we have contributed to it. One can at times note those who have become consistent contributors for they tend to have an amiable cheerfulness. It is not just that they find a pleasure in performing tasks for others or in doing them well: they also seem to have found happiness.

September 2003

Growing pains

It is hard enough to accept our First Principle[7] of the "Fatherhood of God" and to acknowledge that there are influences and occurrences in our lives that cannot be put down to the random chances of an unkind or indifferent fate and that Shakespeare's comment "there is a destiny that shapes our ends, rough-hew them how we will" rings all too truly, but it seems even harder for many to accept that the Fatherhood does not permit us to remain children, and fairly baby-ish children at that.

Childhood and immaturity cannot have been intended as life-long or eternity-long states of existence for beings that have minds with remarkable powers of perception and creative thought. Maturity, conversely, indicates the completion of an educative process or programme that leads to balanced and creative judgements based on a true understanding of our being and circumstances and represents a proper use of those powers.

I cannot support or condone the fatalist schools of life that repetitively intone the mantras "It's my karma and I can do nothing about it", or "my birth sign says that I have these limiting traits in my personality." Sorry, but my Spiritualist philosophy is going to say that your circumstances have placed you in an instructive situation and that you should seek to learn all you can from them. The philosophy continues to the effect that the circumstances will continue to recur until you have made some headway on the learning front.

Shakespeare's concept of destiny seems to imply that there are aims and purposes and that it is intended that we should undergo certain experiences. In this respect I presume that the

---

[7] The Seven Principles of Spiritualism are described in the Appendix on page 84

Fatherhood intends that we should grow up and that what we see as destiny is His being a responsible parent and being kind to us. Though you may find that use of the word "kind" a little too sweeping for comfort.

Where I do have some reservations is in our use of the term Fatherhood, for I feel that to be largely an archaic precedent that neglects the feminine aspects of life; but I have to admit that Parenthood doesn't seem to quite fit the bill either. Perhaps we need to get entirely away from concepts based on physical life.

So if your life is hurting, you may have to ask yourself two questions: What am I trying to learn? What am I failing to understand?

January 2004

Going my way?

Our Seven Principles[8] are generally so in agreement with the tenets and commandments of other belief systems that it always surprises me that we seem so distanced from them. I could add that the distance is largely maintained at their insistence, but I'm never going to accept any ruling that denies the possibilities of happiness and enjoying life.

Accepting responsibility for our own happiness, or the lack of it, is actually an opportunity to make a choice; but it has to be an informed choice made with an understanding of what's at issue. A new way of looking might begin by asking what would make us happy, and happiness must be defined as a freedom from burdensome care rather than a mere indulgence in pleasures.

If you are going to keep a burden on your shoulders, then know that it is there because of a sense of duty or achievement for bearing it. Duty is sometimes placed on us by others who use our willingness as a way of off-loading what should have been their responsibility. Your responsibility, meanwhile, extends to reviewing the situation and making any necessary adjustments.

Being carefree is far from being irresponsible and allies to having taken the right measures to ensure a best possible outcome, after which, one can deem it to be "done and dusted" so that it doesn't become an everyday burden.

Neither does enjoying life, my second requirement, require a daily duty of doing things that promote a sense of well-being. Much can be gained from a greater appreciation of the positive

---

[8] See page 84

and beautiful that surrounds us, for we all have some access to the open air, the sky and our natural surroundings. We can also find a quiet joy in the positive changes in the lives of those we know as we see them gain social and creative skills to enhance their lives.

An alternative definition of happiness might include being in the right place at the right time. Well enough, you could say, but a more serious philosophical view would suggest that Life has provided an opportunity for you to achieve something fulfilling. You may find that unpalatable, but you are in the right place, and this is the right time (it's actually the only time you've got). Yes, I know that your ego is seeking other gratifications, but the soul, through your unconscious mind, has guided you to where you are. And if I say "sorry about that" it's only my ego seeking the gratification of your acceptance.

May 2004

I'm alright, Jack

Many religions, particularly western ones, have long insisted that only their own members will be admitted to that part of the next world commonly called heaven and such an arbitrary judgment is claimed to come from an all-wise, all-understanding, all-forgiving and all-loving God. The more humorous among the cynics have demonstrated their own unsuitability by asserting that "if heaven is going to be that empty, I don't want to go there anyway".

If we are all to continue to claim knowledge of God's wishes and intentions for the world, might it not be better if we were to refrain from endowing Him with so many human traits? I'm sure that we grossly flatter ourselves when we assume that His motivations are as partisan and spiteful as our own.

Surely the time has come when we must accept that our planet is now so populated and the demands for basic resources and the pressures on the environment are such that we must consider the survival of not only "endangered" species but also our own? The Brotherhood of Man and equality under the Fatherhood of God cannot remain high-minded principles to which we pay lip-service when it suits our arguments. They must become the basis of all our considerations and plans for the future.

We must be prepared to extend not only good wishes and respect for other modes of life; we must also offer help where it is needed, without imposing self-seeking conditions. We may even find that circumstances require that sacrifices on our part might have to be made.

I concede that I am writing these thoughts in the comfort of European civilization and that sacrifice has never been a popular word; but the bad news now travels even faster, and neighbour (just another word) now means many more people than it used to.

It's time we started asking "Are you alright, Jack?"

September 2004

Some good may yet come of it

We are still too stunned by the loss of life and widespread devastation to appreciate the full scale of the disaster[9], for only flying over that part of Asia could impress it on our senses, and we are left trying to rationalise the seemingly incomprehensible.

The newspapers have gone beyond the factual reporting of the disaster and have found space on their pages to challenge the leaders of the various religions to "justify" what many would consider to be an Act of God. The challenge is based on two premises: the first being that God is a (super) person, and the second that somebody (anybody) should be held accountable.

Both premises stem from our earliest dawning awareness as human beings and may even be based on the negative instinctive responses of fear and retaliation.

Much of our knowledge of history and geology reminds us that both we and the planet are restless and occasionally given to abrupt and even violent changes, and that there seems a natural part of a physical life that also allows all living things to change and develop; and even progress towards an expanded and more profound future. Personal risk and elements of danger may be the grains of sand that provoke the world as oyster to produce pearls of heroism and compassion, and surely the disaster has brought forth those.

It is a tenet of Spiritualism that we incarnate into this physical and material plane of life to learn through experience,

---

[9] This refers to the Indian Ocean earthquake and tsunami that occurred on 26 December 2004, killing almost 230,000 people

and that as we are often complacent and indolent the experiences that are necessary for our education have at times to be thrust upon us. I freely acknowledge that to think that disasters such as the tsunami may have a purpose is deeply challenging, but if we would believe that the universe and life and evolution have purpose, then disasters must have purpose too.

Although we make great efforts to render all aspects of life safer and more comfortable, the natural world seems to circumvent our precautions. You may choose either to view life as having purpose or as a succession of random meaningless occurrences. I choose to support your right to make that choice.

January 2005

Are you thinking what I'm thinking?

We can't always be sure that what we hope to achieve will eventually come to fruition and it is an inherent part of life that we have to struggle with uncertainty. We might think that we have arranged matters to suit our hopes and aspirations, but so often an unexpected thing makes it impossible for us to attain our goal.

It is natural, at one level, to feel disappointment and even anger towards those who seem to have caused the upset to our plans, but often at some later date we can appreciate that what we had intended would not have been the right thing for us and that matters have not turned out too badly after all. It has to be admitted that we may have to adopt a more spiritually aware standpoint to perceive the "turned out for the best" appreciation, but if the whole purpose of life is an attempt to gain greater spiritual awareness then we should have expected that anyway.

Of course we have some choice in the whole of the aspirations – actions – setbacks – disappointment scenario. Encouraged by worldly values, the desire for creature comforts and manufacturers' insistence that without their products we will fail to have the respect of our peers, we are easily led into an assumption that if we have made our personal environment more ostentatious then we have made the world a better place and that we can then ignore what is occurring outside the boundaries of our material life.

If, however, you do have a pricking sensation in your conscience, or some vague wish to express a spiritual dimension in your life, you will have to accept that it is more than just an expression of your own mind and that you have become an agent working for Providence, God, or even the common weal (I leave you to rate the value of what you do) and that your personal preferences will not then be paramount.

If your sense of compassion towards the world (and you will know whether it is real or just feigned because you believe the world expects it of you) begins with a more affable manner and occasional kind words, it will be enough to at least signal that you have taken the important step of choosing to work with the world for the betterment and progress of all, rather than competing to secure your own individual status at the expense of others.

The concept of free will can be over-conceived, but there is a choice: a choice that I believe could change your life more profoundly than you might initially appreciate.

May 2005

What have you been trying to tell me?

It is a sad characteristic of the human race that we so easily forget in moments of stress that we have aspects of immortality and more lasting purposes than ensuring a roof, a pillow and another meal.

When we are calm we can all accept that this plane of life is a school (usually of hard knocks) and that we are here to learn from each other, but if attacked with even "friendly" advice we respond out of our animal instincts and attack in our turn. Thus we end up with at least two people generating negative energies and doing no good at all not only to each other, but to themselves as well.

The unsubtle thing about the school of life is that you are required to learn the lessons that life has thoughtfully provided for you; and if you prove negligent and fail to grasp the lessons, they will be brought back time and time again until you have demonstrated that you can act as a loving and positive being. Please understand that I am not branding you a failure, just trying to remind you that we are in this together, all of us!

Of course the first question that springs to mind is: who are the teachers? Well, I have already said that we are learning from each other, but in any situation that still leaves the further question: who is teacher and who is pupil? The rub is that we don't know, we all feel that we are in the right of the matter and that they are learning from us, but that may just be our little egos talking.

I can only suggest that the next time you find yourself involved in what one of my friends would call a lively discussion, you should ask yourself two questions: am I being a good teacher? and: am I being a good pupil? Life being what it is, you're probably both playing both roles, for we still seem to have so much to learn that there is the opportunity for both to teach.

In between lessons we can hopefully treat life as a break-time when we can make friends, play with our pals and learn our games and polish our social skills, so that next time we think we have to play as teacher we can do so more lovingly and skillfully.

Class dismissed, and don't forget to do your homework!

September 2005

My brother's keeper, my keeper's brother

The primary and most easily observed characteristic of life is that it changes, endlessly; and we, both as individuals and as nations hurry endlessly in an attempt to keep up with it.

We seem swept along towards an unguessable future while we struggle to maintain order and stability in our lives, often feeling that we are victims of wayward circumstances. However, we are at the same time members of the social order that determines so many of these circumstances.

We may well pay lip-service to concepts of equality and fairness, but limitation and conditions are normally promptly applied; and if they're applied by those we have appointed to determine and apply such conditions then we are not exonerated. Silent acquiescence does not reverberate through hallowed halls.

Not only do we seem to be assuming levels of material well-being that seemingly cannot be sustained, we have for perhaps the first time in the earth's history reached a level of resource demand that the planet itself cannot sustain. Water and hydro-carbons are already points of international tension, and profligate consumerism has become so every-day that we see it as normal and even reasonable.

Just as scientists proclaim, some with pride, that we know more about space and the rest of the solar system than we know about the inner details of our own planet; so too, we have made far more progress in our outer material lives than we have in our inner spiritual lives.

Spiritual progress should perhaps be measured by the yardstick of the poem about Abou Ben Adhem (may his tribe increase!) who explained to the Recording Angel that though he did not greatly love God, he did at least love his fellow men, and was duly placed at the head of the list of those who did love God.

One has only to glance at a newspaper to conclude that we are not generally doing too well in Abou's league table, when the papers with the greatest sales are those that not only invite your envy, jealousy and lust on just about every page, but also demand that you hate someone of their choosing.

I forgot to note the author recently quoted as writing that "hate never resolved hate, only love does that", but I think it worth re-quoting. Neither nostalgia nor community spirit are what they used to be, and a Neighbourhood Watch Scheme is the only time we talk of "our street". The good old days were pretty awful for most people except for those diamonds in the dirt, that we had greater mutual trust and a stronger sense of community. We may have to dig deep within ourselves to find such jewels again.

January 2006

The Spiritualist Party manifesto

Today I am canvassing on behalf of the Spiritualist Party. As only some 21% of people voted in the local elections[10], there must still be plenty who would vote for a truly democratic world where justice, reason and goodwill prevail.

It will obviously be a long time yet before we become sufficient in number to take a leading role in the establishment of such a way of life, but we must prepare for that role by demonstrating our principles of goodwill and respect held equally for all.

Nothing less than a new world-order should herald and celebrate the coming Aquarian Age. Recorded world history has been an endless saga of competing religions, competing armies, competing nations and competing economies; and the cost of all this competition has been nothing but loss: the loss of happiness, loss of freedom, loss of culture, the needless loss of millions and millions of lives and the despoilment and contamination of the planet.

We have reached the point where the climate of competition is damaging the climate of the planet itself, and it is no longer realistic to either deny the environmental damage or easily reverse it. Increasing populations with their demands for improving standards of living can only predicate increased competition for the planet's resources of water, food and energy.

Must we go yet further down the road of competitiveness and its attendant losses? Surely we can come to the point of

---

[10] Local elections took place in England (only) on 4 May 2006

agreeing that we will not only share all material things equally, but we will also ensure their availability for future generations.

I do not think that we can leave these now urgent contradictions to the politicians and scientists, for I do not see how they can re-invent water, not even out of the somewhat polluted air, and the widespread enthusiasm for re-cycling surely demonstrates an underlying anxiety and un-ease in many of the population.

Burying our heads in the sand will not answer the problem; though by the time the planet has largely turned to desert, sand may be the only commodity in abundance!

May 2006

Something to celebrate

We all too easily let the days slip one into another and, before we know it, yet another week has gone by and we then lose the sense of purpose and achievement in our lives. Sameness and boredom sap our energies and stifle our imaginations, and so we need a shake-up to sharpen our appreciation of what is happening in our lives.

The proposal "let's have a party" should not just be viewed as frivolous escapism, for the opportunity to create an occasion with all the associated memories that can be recalled later will give a significance to an event.

My thoughts spring from more than our celebration of Ealing Church's Centenary[11], for I feel that we need to celebrate our individual progress and achievements. Greetings cards can now be obtained for many different occasions and anniversaries, but I have yet to find a card for becoming more caring and considerate or for having learnt about life.

Today, encouraged by the media, it is the fashion to revel in the failings and indiscretions of newsworthy or publicity-seeking people, whereas good deeds either go unreported or are done anonymously for fear of ridicule – all this at a time when encouragement and helping hands are needed at least as much as ever.

We all have needs from society and beyond the material necessities of a home and a modest income we also hope to receive respect, consideration and some warmth and affection in personal relationships. These last human needs are only

---

[11] September 2006 marked 100 years since the church had been founded and a Service of Re-dedication was held with accompanying celebrations.

available to the extent that others are ready to provide them for us; and equally, they are only available to others to the extent that *we* are prepared to offer them.

I believe in the value of community participation, not only because it provides support where that is needed, but even more because it provides opportunities for us to express the best of ourselves and to find higher aspects of our being.

We can celebrate that the community of our church has persisted for a hundred years. We can celebrate that we are the present members of it. We can celebrate that so many of the members are our friends and that our community will continue for a second century.

September 2006

At sixes and sevens

Our natural world seems increasingly to reflect our own turmoil and confusion. Roses are still bravely flowering-on as if 2006 was never coming to an end, while the newspapers daily report of lambs being born and plants springing back into life earlier in 2007 than tradition dictates.

The media seem to delight in keeping us all in a state of perplexed confusion. On the one hand we are required to vote in endless trivial polls as to who should be given an award for making a public fool of themselves and on the other, we are advised what to eat, what to wear, what to see, read or listen to, so as to not appear as public fools ourselves.

Do we have so little sense of ourselves that we cannot make up our own minds as to who and what we are? This fear of being ourselves in a world where individuality is something that should be cherished and encouraged, but often isn't, smacks of a state of everlasting juvenility. If we are afraid of being different, it is because we instinctively know that the crowd hates those who think for themselves; but being called "smarty-pants" is at least an acknowledgment that you have intelligence.

If there is any purpose in Creation, and the whole point of being a Spiritualist is that you definitely think there is, then surely that purpose includes some concept of progress. A passing consideration of any fellow human being (unless you're head-over-heels in love with them) will suggest, as the famous landscape gardener was wont to observe "a capability for improvement". Nerds see no point in athletics and athletes see no point in improving brain power – one must therefore assume that *both* must be developed.

With Christmas over to the point where you're already no longer sure who gave you each present and New Year resolutions are just a wistful memory, it can be fairly assumed that you have made a transition to 2007. You doubtless brought some emotional baggage with you, but do check whether this still represents you as you are now, or if it only echoes the old you of a year ago.

In life it is still true that he who travels light travels fast; so know what your life's journey is about and try to avoid being led too far astray by those eager to offer advice.

January 2007

In terms of life

If one can think beyond the basic proposition that “life is painful, therefore it is a punishment” and yet still feel in need of some justification or sense of purpose, then Spiritualist philosophy might be the thing for you: a philosophy that earthly life is the “school of experience” and that what we learn adds to the progress and development of our eternal spirits.

Mind you, far from everyone accepts that we have (or are) eternal spirits. The hedonistic enjoyment of earthly pleasures is certainly a lot of fun, but often seems to be pursued with both an eagerness and a need for repetition that border on desperation and the problem with repetition is that it ultimately leads to boredom.

Change does seem implicit in any concept of life (hopefully in a positive direction); and this modern life, with all its assumed advantages, seems to demand ever-increasing change in us as the social, moral and even environmental pressures pile up.

We do have some ability to respond: we can either change the troublesome circumstances or our attitude to them, in our earthly or eternal minds; that last course being our entire reason for being on the earth in the first place. All of which indicates that we are required to take responsibility for our own lives; and incidentally, that we should not take unnecessary responsibility for the lives of others.

The concept that we are children of a divine all-creating Father God is widely held, and I would add the condition that He requires us to grow to maturity, for I cannot envisage an eternity surrounded by petulant, demanding spiritual teenagers (sorry about that, kids!)

My quiet observation of life leads me to the notion that there is a gentle intelligence trying to untangle the knots in our lives and I think of it as being a form of divine providence. At the same time I also notice that many people seem driven to make changes in their lives that add to their responsibilities and stress, without giving them any lasting happiness, but maybe that is just how we organize our lessons.

Learning not to interfere with that divine providence might be one such lesson.

May 2007

How to win enemies and influence people

The outcome of any experiment becomes a part of experience. This relationship applies not only in the world of science, because life in any form, and specifically our experience of it, can be considered as a continuing experiment. If so, we should then ask: what is the experiment of which we are a part? Our detailed historical knowledge is limited to such a recent and brief period of the whole story that it may be that the experiment drifted away from its original intention too early for us to now notice a change.

Can it be that the Divinity that initiated Creation, and our creation too, intended that we should use our technological advances to despoil our planetary home and give us the ability to express personal, ethnic and national enmities with ever greater violence? I do not think that most people hold that those were the Divinity's intentions, but they have, by default, become the intentions of too many individuals and too many nations.

The default (actually our fault) is that we have taught ourselves over many generations that the God we venerate as the source of all wisdom and love is a God to be feared. It was long ago decided that gods (and God) could be swayed by sacrifices and fulsome praise to change the natural order of the created universe (i.e. our lives) to suit our desires for power, prosperity and pleasure, all at the expense of others.

How can we relate the positive and life-enhancing values that we believe of God, and believe to be the potential within ourselves, to the violence and materialism that fills our newspapers? I think that we are fighting a long battle and must include resolution and fortitude in our defence and demonstrate by example that we are able to live fulfilled and happy lives without needing to appropriate excessive material possessions and without having another's blood on our conscience.

To be a fundamentally happy person is to be the envy of others and to be a constant reminder that their lives seriously lack a sense of fulfillment. The truth prevails because all else declines; your truth should be a sustainable happiness.

September 2007

Between the two worlds

It's January, and as our New Year's resolutions fall to the floor almost as rapidly as the pine needles from our Christmas trees, normality is re-established. Such a pity, really, because last year's normality wasn't all that wonderful, and we had hoped for something better.

The difficulty is that we decided to try to be more attractive and likeable to other people, without really knowing what it is that they dislike; but in the end *you* more or less like yourself, so your heart was never in it anyway.

The real changes that we make in our lives are those that come to us because we have learnt a new and better way to live our lives that has put us in greater harmony with the universe and the part we are to play in it.

Spiritualism's first aim is to demonstrate and prove that the human spirit survives beyond this physical life – it's up to you to work on the proof, which should at least provoke a few questions of the "what does that mean for me?" variety. Well, what it does mean for you is that you can become a construction worker in no less a project than continuing the creation of the universe by using the energies that Life brings to you for that very purpose.

Do not think that our planet is just a mindless ball of rock and water that has no aims, intentions, or dreams. "The stuff of this world is mind stuff" was said by a great British scientist[12], not some bearded and woolly-headed day dreamer. So if you

---

[12] Attributed to Sir Arthur Eddington, British astrophysicist (1882-1944)

are prompted to some small kindly action, try to remember that it's the mind of this part of creation that is asking you to do it.

Do not look for rewards; they will come, but not in response to your desires. Prove yourself a consistent helper, and you will get promoted to bigger tasks, and feel a greater sense of purpose and satisfaction in life, and if that ultimately leads to your greater happiness, than I'm happy for you.

Have a good year!

January 2008

From Russia, with love

Life is like a Russian doll of paradoxes, in that the main challenge of our lives is to discover the purpose in our lives. It does seem innate in the human mind to seek justification for our actions, and to endeavour to find some sense that we are participating in the affairs of the universe and not just acting out a meaningless charade of domestic chores and self-indulgent pleasure/leisure diversions to distract us away from the sense of ennui that seems ever to lurk on the boundaries of our consciousness.

The only way that I have found to escape from this sense of ennui is to escape from attention to myself into an awareness of the needs and wants of other people. While at the same time accepting that every person has the right to conduct their life as they see fit, we can perhaps provide some information, thought, or helping hand that enables them to take a step in life that they might not have otherwise achieved. Take no great sense of virtue in having done that because you have done no more than Life has required of you to support your justification for the continuation of your own life.

Of course, to open a Russian doll is only to find a similar doll within the first, but when seeking purpose within one's life, that may represent a move into a world within a world, providing a shift to a new understanding. In the universe of the mind, worlds tend to be within worlds rather than be spaced out at great physical distances from each other: a convenient difference for those of us confined within physical bodies. This apparent shift to an inner world has the effect that we can be moving towards the centre of our own psychological and spiritual being and moving towards a greater understanding of ourselves; and as we are each a part of the phenomenon of life we can presume that we are gaining a greater understanding of life itself. This may prove to be very close to the purpose behind all our lives.

The next question should probably be: "what indications do we receive from a closer awareness of life?" All indications that have come to my attention are that we should seek to support each other's efforts in the search of understanding; encouraging, inspiring and energising with our positive thoughts, and I presume that such positive thoughts are no less than an expression of the universal love that we are required to express towards each other. You may not feel it as love, because we tend to associate love with the expression of great emotional feeling of attraction towards another specific person, but the recognition that we are a part of the human race and a cousin of all forms of life may actually be the highest that we can achieve.

Eastern philosophers spoke of the great secret concealed by being on display everywhere, and vital though we generally feel the sense of sight to be, we also have the ability to see only that which appears to align with our concepts and prejudices. We may, therefore, remain blind to the potential and beauty that our lives contain and never realize the great secret.

May 2008

Here and now

Ancient religions, particularly the eastern ones, have stressed the importance of awareness and being conscious of all that is happening around one. This has been given various names and "living in the moment" is perhaps the most commonly recognised and understood.

If "living in the moment" does represent awareness of the whole of life, then we are too often very good at avoiding it. Too many of us (and I include myself) have been overly taught by anxious parents that we must not only behave respectfully but must always put the desires of others before our own needs. This may be fine for maintaining an ordered society, but it does so at the cost of much personal disappointment and failure to achieve potentials. We should perhaps learn to consider ourselves as of equal importance to those whom we have been taught to defer to.

Many burdened in these ways live by an inherited set of rules for almost every aspect of life and of course these rules also project onto individual futures. The "here and now" that we should be living in for our enhanced awareness is crushed almost to nothing between the two great masses of past teaching and projected future expectations, and we may have to fight for our awareness to prevent its being squashed out of all existence. We will then be fighting to be our real selves and not just the persons that our mentors would like us to be.

In Spiritualism it is customary to view life as an educational training with many opportunities to learn through experiences; not only one's own, but also through those of others. Given that we tend to cautiousness, we perhaps have fewer experiences than would allow us to achieve all our potential.

Life must be construed as an adventure, and we must summon up a little courage to go out and live it, because sitting in the corner mumbling “please don’t hurt me” looks like a wasted opportunity. “Here and now” defines the life that the universe is currently offering you, so don’t, please, waste it.

September 2008

A window on the world

I moved house last summer and the view from my window looks onto a wildlife park – tall trees under which the nettles and brambles wage their ancient and endless battle for territorial supremacy. Not much in the way of neat grass verges to the path that runs through it all.

During the summer the foliage concealed the path, but now I can see the people walking their dogs, cycling to work, or just enjoying being out in the sunshine and fresh air.

So I now have a home that I'm happy to live in and that also provides a metaphor for my stage in life, in that I am myself in the autumn of life and can now see others travelling their paths of experience. Some dedicate their time to the well-being of others, some seek to express their sense of purpose and yet others savour the beauty of the physical world and the warmth of friendship and relationship.

It is not my role in life to judge who is doing the right thing, who is being lackadaisical, or who is being outrightly selfish or dishonest, unless my opinion is asked by that person. It is only my role to look out of the window and watch the spectacle of life as it travels along the path.

The Native Americans talked of walking in another man's moccasins before passing judgment, so I remind myself that Life is the teacher and that Life will provide the guidance and the lessons to bring each person to a greater understanding and to an appreciation of their role in a gentle re-building of the world into a harmonious unity.

Patience is an early and necessary lesson and I hope that you will forgive my asking how long it has taken you to reach your present level of understanding – and are you entitled to expect everyone else to be quicker?

January 2009

A New Pair of Eyes

The woodland path that I wrote of in the last newsletter is again veiled by a new season's fresh foliage that I find refreshing to my eyes and soothing to my mind, and I reflect that our earliest ancestors lived in a green world of forests and grasslands, whereas we are surrounded by urban colours that (over)stimulate us. Little wonder perhaps that so many feel stressed and little wonder too that gardening has become such a popular pastime.

The wood still provides the odd metaphor, for although my eyes are less sharp, I now see nuances because I look for longer. There are two ash trees, one majestic and mature and another, doubtless seeded from the old one and little more than half its height, but more vigorous and leafing up at least two weeks earlier than its parent. I recognise the more measured approach that comes from having endured so many summers and winters.

In the course of a church service it is frequent enough that we are reminded that we are "spirit now" and not just when we have departed this earthly plane and I look around and wonder how many have fully realised that we are here to teach each other and learn from each other and that we have the common experience of the journey to understanding that makes us truly brothers and sisters. That realisation gives us another and new pair of eyes that look with compassion and sympathy instead of judgment and rejection. One has then grown spiritually and felt the urge to help another upon their journey.

Hardly surprising then, that one tends to see these new eyes more often in older folk who can greet each other with the wry smile that acknowledges the found wisdom and scars that record the other's life journey. Been there and done that? Certainly, and a cupboard full of tee-shirts to prove it! Some still looking pristine (didn't really like the person, or didn't feel comfortable in the situation), some very worn and some even with tear stains or the blood from accidents or the surgeon's healing knife.

As Kahlil Gibran suggested, perhaps through such eyes God smiles upon the world[13].

May 2009

---

[13] The original quote reads "Through the hands of such as these God speaks, and from behind their eyes He smiles upon the earth." Kahlil Gibran *The Prophet*

Darwin and all that stuff

A centenary celebration is usually a good time for raking over the ashes of an old quarrel, for originally it was not a polite debate and this time it has still produced enough sparks to roast the old chestnuts all over again. It may be 200 years since Charles Darwin's birth and 150 years since the publication of *On the origin of species*, but the old polarisations and enmities still exist. The mutual antagonism between science and religion must have started a very long time ago and by now the situation has reached an intractable stalemate, so an out-of-the-box-thinking approach might provide a useful solution.

My own modest explorations of philosophy and speculative thought have led me to the useful supposition that when faced with two or more mutually contradictory concepts then there must be an over-arching perception that allows those concepts to co-exist. Then one has only to concentrate one's efforts on finding the over-arching bit to resolve the impasse; and if I make that sound easy, then it's only to keep the path clearly visible.

Where I start to bang the drum for Spiritualism is that we seem to be in a privileged position, being outside the norms of both orthodox science and orthodox religion and constrained by neither. We are free, therefore, to explore concepts that might enable us to find a rationale that suits both our experience of this plane of life and our understanding of the hereafter and also resolve the contradictory paradox problem.

Darwin's theory seems well supported by evidence going back more than several hundred million years, but we see little evolution in the short term, as change generally comes about from environmental pressures and we are not (as yet) in a time of pressure.

However, as Spiritualists, we are also aware that the unseen world does sometimes seek to bring beneficial changes to this plane of life and some of them, though small, could have had far-reaching consequences. I am thinking here of the surprising change several thousand years ago when a type of grass changed from scattering its seed to retaining it on the stalk – a change that would seem to have ensured its extinction without the early interventions of harvesting and sowing and all this not too long before the time when the increasing human population would need new forms of food.

So I believe in evolution and I also believe in an intelligent creative intervening force, and although this puts me at some odds with both sides of the controversy, I feel that it is the rational view for a Spiritualist. I do not seek to be different just to strike a pose, but neither of the two concepts seems sufficient on its own.

September 2009

Knowing me, knowing you, and knowing God

Those of us who think about such matters tend to agree that humans derive emotional support and security from a repertoire of self-sustained illusions. We present a personality to the world that partly presents what we require of the world and also partly what we think the world requires of us.

"People can't stand too much reality" is not a new observation and it seems to remain as valid as when first said. Certainly modern life offers so many distractions from the mundane world – the cult of celebrity, the music that effectively drowns out all ordinary sound, and the rap lyrics that aggressively speak so largely in terms of violence and anger.

Our materialistic society conditions us to accept that only success in a material sense is of value. Young people have often expressed the desire to become "celebrities" or other publicly recognised figures, and self-respect no longer seems sufficient reward for the modern personality.

It may be that where respect is no longer accorded to other people and where their self-respect is not confirmed by those around them, people have to seek other forms of self-esteem.

"When everybody's somebody, then no-one's anybody" wrote W.S. Gilbert for one of the G & S operettas, so do we really need public labels for self-respect? I think not, but what I do think is that our self-esteem should be based on our self-evaluation and not subject to the fluctuating opinions of others who are scrambling to bolster their own self-esteem and not ours. So we must learn to judge ourselves fairly and not with the critical eyes of those who feel the need to think themselves superior.

As Spiritualists, if we really believe our own teachings, we should accept that we all fulfil a function in the great complex drama of human life and being parts of that drama we cannot truly gain an outside and objective view.

Only Spirit can have that objective view and only Spirit can objectively evaluate our words and deeds. What we know of God, and that can only be the aspects of which we are aware, is largely that He is more loving and generous than we are.

January 2010

Life and change

We tend to classify any object as being alive if it exhibits some form of change, either of shape or position, but generally movement does seem a necessary requirement. So why then are we so often reluctant to accept change in our own lives? “Do I have to change?” is a frequent response, even from those whose present conditions seem unacceptable to the rest of us.

Fear of an unknown future causes us to cling to existing circumstances even when we have a possibility of improvement, and even a challenge of “how often has the very worst outcome to a situation occurred in your life?” fails to elicit a more positive reaction.

Every Spiritualist church service includes messages from loved ones that they are working to achieve a satisfactory outcome to difficult situations in our lives, and philosophical teachings too state that difficulties are placed on our paths so that we might learn to overcome them and gain wisdom from such experiences.

It is the fear of the unknown future that stifles our ambition and effectively suffocates our lives. After all, is that much unknown? Yes, we will live lives of longer or shorter duration; yes, we will experience the pain of diseases and the pain of the loss of loved ones, and finally experience the mortality of our physical bodies. All these things we were born for and are natural to our lives.

The unknown is of course the not knowing or accepting that we have a continuing life as spirits, and indeed that we are spirits now, undergoing an educational process and that, at the end of schooling, the toys of material life will be put back in the cupboard. In not having a belief one effectively turns the purpose and meaning of life upside down, and this effectively turns the appreciation of life upside down, so people can't be sure if they're on their heads or their heels.

So if you have no fixed star or purpose in your life, get a philosophy, either ours, or a better one if you can find it – in which case, come back and tell me.

May 2010

Flattery will get you nowhere

The witticism that "If God made Man in his own image, then Man returned the compliment" gains its humour from the wisdom that all pearls have an uncomfortable grit of truth within them.

All the recorded history of mankind, though not the unrecorded history of God, has allotted to all gods the virtues and (particularly) the frailties of humans; and apparently God, and the pagan gods too, were given to expressing anger, wrath, jealousy, greed, lust and a desire for revenge. "The gods are angry and we must placate them by killing something or someone" is the basic plot of many Greek tragedies and other legends.

Thus we as Spiritualists find it difficult to align our Divine Source with the teachings of other religions and find our best relationships with philosophies that do not denigrate our "Source of all Love" with the frailties mentioned above. Neither do we seek blanket forgiveness for the errors that we ourselves have committed during our lives. Rather, we accept that we have, or should have, learned something from our experiences at the hands of other people and, hopefully, that they have learned from us.

We value this concept of life being an educational process because what we have learned becomes the basis for our personal philosophy, which is that God not only helps those who help themselves, but also those who seek to help others.

We "understand", and I qualify the word, that the Divinity is all-seeing and all-knowing, and therefore appreciates all qualities both good and bad in their balancing opposites, while remaining at the tranquil centre of the storms of life. I cannot therefore believe that he is swayed either by expressions of fulsome praise or self-seeking prayers of the “grant me fame and fortune” variety.

Perhaps the Bible should have said: “By the intention of your deeds shall ye be known”.

September 2010

A New Year revolution

After giving the matter a little thought, I have come to the realisation that revolutions and resolutions do have quite a lot in common, for both express a wish beneficially to change a situation in which people are feeling oppressed.

Where both often seem to go awry is that they are in their different ways triggered by ill-balanced states of mind. Revolutions often come from over-intellectualised considerations, and resolutions from an excess of heartfelt wanting.

With revolutions it's usually the extremists who win the day and soon start imposing their rigid ideologies on a population that had been told they were fighting for freedom. Resolutions may be a different matter, but there is still a war being fought and this time it's inside the person and it's between the head and the heart. The head well knows that (for instance) smoking is not a healthy habit, but the heart can so eloquently plead that "it's not doing that much harm" and that it does help the person to relax, so that often the heart wins the argument because the narrow neck regions of the body seem to apply some restriction to the force of the brain's arguments.

With failed resolutions the situation returns to very nearly the "before we started" state, but with revolutions the matter is often different. Win or lose, a lot of people will have lost their security, their homes and in many cases even their lives for the idealistic cause that initiated the revolution, but which has since become a tyranny.

With failure being the most probable outcome of both resolutions and revolutions, it may be time for a re-think, and it's my think that, as none of us is a perfectly integrated person with head and heart working in harmony, we will all have to find peace within ourselves rather than the continuing restless belligerence between those two influential areas.

If we really wish to change our lives for the better, we must employ all our abilities and skills. The heart must really want it and the head must be given time to plan the change and list all the resources and supports that we might need.

So, if you're still in too much of a hurry to digest my letter, then at least engage heart, mind and spirit before making a resolution; and never, ever, start a revolution.

January 2011

A time to reap and a time to sow

In this modern life, where the world is largely seen via the television, the spring season is heralded by the gentle patter of seed and plant catalogues landing on doormats and is for many of us the way we recognise the start of another year.

We are often no more aware of the seasons in our own lives and fail to recognise the inner changes that indicate that we have moved on to a newer understanding or awareness; or that we have "let go" of a grievance or grudge that has rankled on and on, causing us to lose appreciation of the blessings of help and beauty that should uplift our lives.

The awful truth that I must now reveal is that Spiritualists are not generally any more spiritual than anyone else. There are no "chosen races" or preferred religions and humanity is living an earthly life in order to experience certain conditions and lessons and thus become wiser. That we seem to have a great reluctance to actually learn and become wiser must by now be fully appreciated in the spirit world.

Much as our guides wish to help us, another unpalatable truth is that the motivation must come from us ourselves. Our jealously-guarded free will can be a bit of a two-edged weapon; and as we still lack wisdom, not all of our decisions will be wise. Any bad decision will initiate another learning programme and thus the endless cycle of experiences continues.

I do not think that the concept of karma as a system of rewards and punishments represents the true life mechanism, nor do I believe that a loving God devises punishments, but I do believe that unpleasant and painful experiences are subtly-devised situations to draw attention to a flaw or lack of humanity in our characters.

So the next time a spiritual seed catalogue lands on your doormat, look through it and look around your spiritual garden and consider any weeds that could be replaced with more beautiful flowers.

Cultivating a more agreeable attitude may seem insincere, but persist and it will naturalise within you. So if you wish to be a more fragrant person, I suggest that you take up soul gardening.

May 2011

Apocalypse later

Predicting the end of the world (and I suppose that our greater understanding of the cosmos means predicting the end of the universe), has been a story of endless failure, for no one has so far made a successful prediction.

All the enthusiasm for prediction has, I suspect, been born of a feeling that earthly life is dissatisfying and seemingly pointless, so let's get it over with, so that we can have a better time in the next world. I see several flaws and assumptions in the concept, in that we assume that all life in the next world will be comparatively blissful. Well, no it won't. All the lessons that we avoided or failed to understand will become more painful, as it will not be just bodily pain but pain of the emotions and mind. Nor can we be so sure what fine people we will seem once our egos have been stripped of their material possessions and self-opinionated illusions, for clothes in the next world may conceal parts of our bodies, but certainly not the state of our souls.

Even the scientists' dreams of reaching and populating other planets seem utopian, but perhaps they're only hoping to escape from the religionists, who insist that the present boundaries of science do not encompass everything. Although I am reassured by the scientists' view that the earth should remain habitable for a very long time yet.

I echo the insurance company's line by saying that we shouldn't turn a disaster into an apocalypse. We should consider that earthly life is only an interlude in the seemingly infinitely long spirit life that we all have, and that the rough and tumble of life on this planet does not predicate the end of the human race. Our descendants will continue to populate (and probably despoil) the earth.

So you can understand that I'm all for the long haul that will take us to greater understanding of ourselves, of all life, and of the greatly unknown future that confronts us. Do not be afraid at that prospect: it's all adventure and some of it could be fun, particularly when we've learned how to live life joyfully.

January 2012

Olympians all

For the ancient Greeks Mount Olympus was the home of their gods: gods that at times exhibited all too human frailties.

Can we not seek to progress in the opposite direction and hope to rise above our frailties and imperfections and become more god-like? Spirit teachers have assured us that this is our ultimate future and have pleaded that we should not unnecessarily delay that progress. Obviously we still have much to learn, and that will take long enough, but we almost wilfully turn away from experiences and opportunities to express the courage and determination that the Olympic athletes have demonstrated[14].

I feel that almost too much has been made of the medal scores at the games. All the competitors did their very best and in other circumstances, doing your very best is accepted as being the greatest achievement possible.

I never managed to run as fast as the slowest of Olympic competitors, but had I competed I would have saved them from coming last and be able to think that in that day I ran with the gods of Olympus.

We already all have one gold medal, that of eternal life. We are all in the human race, but we only have to compete against ourselves and be able on occasions to say, that on that day I did my very best.

September 2012

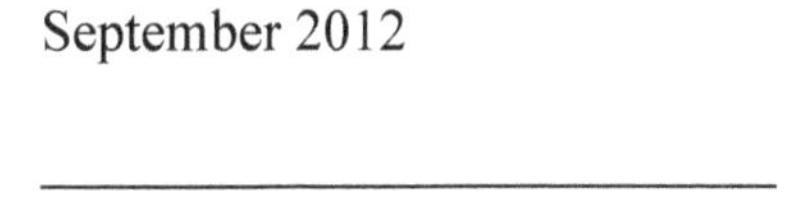

[14] The Summer Olympics had taken place in London in July/August 2012

Appendix:
The Seven Principles of Spiritualism

Emma Hardinge Britten (1823-1899) was born in London and worked throughout the English-speaking world as a medium, speaker and pioneer of the Spiritualist movement from the 1850s onwards. Over the many years of her work she developed a set of principles which she stated were given to her through her mediumship by the spirit world.

Early versions vary in their numbers and wording, but they were adopted in their present form by the Spiritualists' National Union (SNU), founded in 1901, and are widely accepted by Spiritualists as a statement of the understanding that underpins their religion.

Richard frequently makes references to them in his articles.

They are:

1. The Fatherhood of God
2. The Brotherhood of Man
3. The communion of spirits and the ministry of angels
4. The continuous existence of the human soul
5. Personal responsibility
6. Compensation and retribution hereafter for all the good and evil deeds done on earth
7. Eternal progress open to every human soul

Further information on the Seven Principles and the history and philosophy of Spiritualism can be found at snu.org.uk.

Ingram Content Group UK Ltd.
Milton Keynes UK
UKHW010633090723
424784UK00001B/2